CAMELS

by Kathryn Stevens

Published in the United States of America by The Child's World®
1980 Lookout Drive • Mankato, MN 56003-1705
800-599-READ • www.childsworld.com

PHOTO CREDITS

© Arco Images/Alamy: 6–7
© blickwinkel/Alamy: 19
© David Curl/naturepl.com: 22
© Dominique Braud/Dembinsky Photo Assoc. Inc.: 26–27
© Doug Allan/naturepl.com: 16–17
© Images of Africa Photobank/Alamy: 21
© Jose Fuste Raga/Corbis: 5
© Klaus Hackenberg/zefa/Corbis: 29
© Konrad Wothe/Minden Pictures: 13
© Picture Contact/Alamy: 24
© Richard T. Nowitz/Corbis: 15
© Shai Ginott/Corbis: 10–11
© SPL/Photo Researchers, Inc.: cover, 1
© Tierbild Okapia/Photo Researchers, Inc.: 9

ACKNOWLEDGMENTS

The Child's World®: Mary Berendes, Publishing Director;
Katherine Stevenson, Editor; Pamela Mitsakos, Photo Researcher;
Judy Karren, Fact Checker

The Design Lab: Kathleen Petelinsek, Design and Page Production

LIBRARY OF CONGRESS CATALOGING-IN-PUBLICATION DATA

Stevens, Kathryn, 1954–
   Camels / by Kathryn Stevens.
       p. cm. — (New naturebooks)
   Includes index.
   ISBN 978-1-59296-844-2 (library bound : alk. paper)
   1. Camels—Juvenile literature. I. Title. II. Series.
   QL737.U54S74 2007
   599.63'62—dc22   2007013414

Table of Contents

On the cover: This camel is keeping its eye on the photographer.

Meet the Camel!

People sometimes call camels "ships of the desert" because of their rolling way of moving. When walking, camels move both left legs, then both right legs.

For centuries, nomadic Bedouins who lived in Middle Eastern and African deserts relied on camels.

The hot sun beats down through the clear desert air. All you can see is lots and lots of sand. Then, off in the distance, some little specks appear. The specks get larger as they get closer. Finally you see that they are animals, with people riding on their backs. The animals are tall. They have long legs, long necks, and huge bumps on their backs. What are these strange-looking creatures of the desert? They're camels!

This man is riding a camel in Egypt.

What Are Camels?

Male camels are bigger than females. A good-sized male might be 7 feet (a little over 2 m) tall at the shoulder and weigh 1,500 pounds (680 kg). The hump usually stands about a foot (30 cm) higher.

Four camel relatives still live in South America—wild guanacos and vicuñas, and domesticated llamas and alpacas.

Camels are large, four-legged **mammals** with woolly hair, long legs and necks, and an amazing ability to live in hot, dry regions. Like other mammals, camels have warm bodies and feed their babies milk from their bodies. But they're best known for the fatty humps on their backs. When food and water are scarce, camels use the fat in their humps as a source of water and energy.

The first camel-like creatures lived in North America some 40 million years ago. They slowly moved into Asia and Africa. Over time, most camel relatives in the Americas died out. But in Asia and Africa, they developed into the camels we know today. In those regions, camels have been kept by people, or **domesticated**, for at least 4,000 years.

The hot desert sun doesn't seem to bother these camels!

Are There Different Kinds of Camels?

In Syria, scientists have found bones of giant camels that are up to 100,000 years old. These huge animals were twice as big as today's camels. In fact, they were as tall as some elephants! Tools have been found with the bones, suggesting that people hunted the camels.

There are two basic kinds of camels, Bactrian (BACK-tree-un) camels and dromedaries (DRAH-muh-der-eez). The two kinds of camels look different and come from different lands.

Bactrian camels have two big humps on their backs. These camels come from the deserts and dry **steppes** of Mongolia and central Asia. These regions can get scorching hot or freezing cold. With their sturdy bodies and long, woolly fur, Bactrian camels are built for these harsh lands. The color of their wool ranges from light to dark brown. Most Bactrians are domesticated, but there are still a few hundred wild ones. The wild Bactrians have shorter hair, slimmer bodies, and smaller humps than the domesticated ones.

You can see the two humps on this Bactrian camel. How does this camel differ from the one on the next page?

Dromedaries, also called Arabian camels, have one big hump in the middle of the back. They come from desert regions of southwest Asia and northern Africa, including the Sahara Desert. They are a little taller and slimmer than Bactrians. Their natural color is light brown, but people have raised them in colors from white to dark brown. All of today's dromedaries come from domesticated camels. The last truly wild dromedaries died out about 2,000 years ago.

By controlling which camels had babies, people have developed many different **breeds** of camels. Some of them are heavier work animals. Some dromedary breeds are slim and built for racing or riding. People have also bred crosses between Bactrians and dromedaries. Some of these crosses are big, sturdy work animals.

How is this dromedary different from the Bactrian camel on page 9?

There's an easy way to keep the two kinds of camels straight. If you turn the first letter of "Bactrian" on its side, it has two humps. If you turn the first letter of "Dromedary" on its side, it only has one hump.

11

How Do Camels Survive the Heat?

Most mammals keep their bodies at a certain temperature. But a camel's body temperature goes up during the daytime heat and down at night.

Camels can sweat, but they hardly ever do. That's one way their bodies save water.

Dromedaries' feet do well on sand but not on sharp rocks, mud, or slippery ground.

Camels are amazingly well adapted to desert life. Thick pads on their knees, elbows, and chests help them rest on hot sand. Their nostrils can close to keep out sand and dust. Thick eyebrows and two rows of long eyelashes keep sand out of their eyes. Their feet have two broad toes with leathery pads on the bottom, wide enough for walking on sand.

The most dangerous thing about the desert is that the heat and dryness cause plants and animals to lose water. If they lose too much water, they can die. Camels hold onto the water in their bodies better than most animals do. And even if they lose one-fourth or more of their body weight in water, they can still stay alive. When they find water again, they soak it up quickly. Scientists are still learning how camels' bodies can do all these things.

Did you ever notice how long camels' back legs look? Most four-legged animals have skin stretched between their upper legs and the sides of their bodies. Camels don't, so their legs look longer. Air moves under their bodies more freely, too, keeping them cooler.

What Do Camels Eat?

When a herd of camels feeds, the animals spread out and eat only a few leaves from each plant. That way they don't destroy the plants that live in these desert regions.

A dromedary's hump can store up to 80 pounds (36 kg) of fat.

Camels use their 34 teeth for ripping and chewing tough plant foods—and for fighting.

Today, many camels eat foods people give them, such as grass, oats, wheat, and sweet dates. But camels that need to find their own food will eat almost any kind of plant—including dry grasses, twigs, and thorny plants other animals don't eat. A camel uses its long, tough tongue and thick, split upper lip to pick leaves off thorn bushes without getting hurt. If food is really scarce, camels will even eat bones, meat, skin, fish, rope, or people's tents!

When camels are well fed, their humps are full and stand straight up. If they start living off the fat in their humps, the humps get smaller and flop to the side. With water and food, the humps plump up again in a few days.

This camel has found a juicy plant to eat in Israel's Negev Desert.

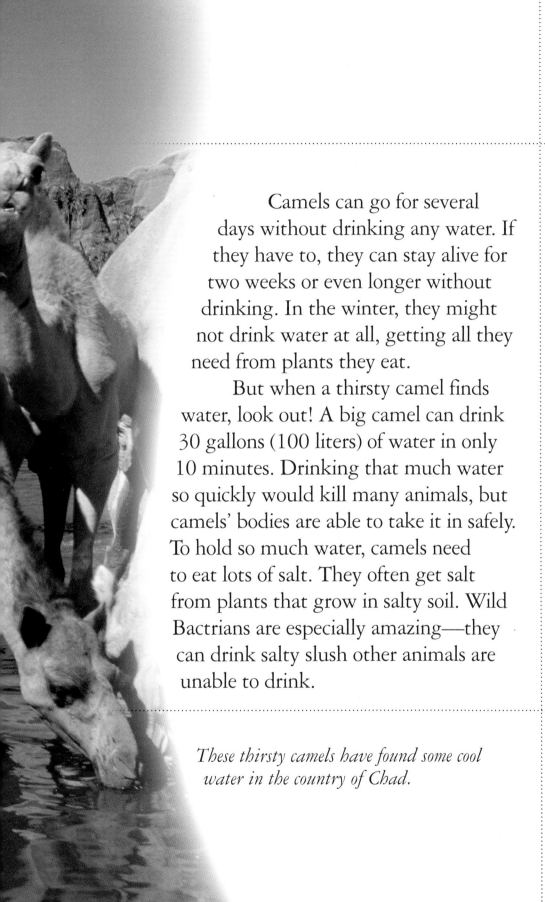

Camels can go for several days without drinking any water. If they have to, they can stay alive for two weeks or even longer without drinking. In the winter, they might not drink water at all, getting all they need from plants they eat.

But when a thirsty camel finds water, look out! A big camel can drink 30 gallons (100 liters) of water in only 10 minutes. Drinking that much water so quickly would kill many animals, but camels' bodies are able to take it in safely. To hold so much water, camels need to eat lots of salt. They often get salt from plants that grow in salty soil. Wild Bactrians are especially amazing—they can drink salty slush other animals are unable to drink.

These thirsty camels have found some cool water in the country of Chad.

Like cows, camels swallow their food, then bring it back up later to chew some more. That's called "chewing their cud."

Camels are known to spit when they are upset. Their "spit" is actually thrown-up stomach contents with some saliva from their mouths.

17

What Are Baby Camels Like?

Baby camels start to get tough, dry pads on their chests, elbows, and knees when they are about five months old.

Many baby dromedaries are born white. Ones with pure white noses and toes stay white. Ones with a little color on their noses and toes get darker.

Female camels are called *cows*. Males are *bulls*.

After a male and female camel mate, the baby grows inside the mother for 12 to 14 months. Camel mothers usually have only one baby at a time. The babies are called **calves**. A camel calf weighs about 80 pounds (37 kg) at birth and can walk the same day.

Camel calves (especially dromedaries) have very long legs! But they don't have humps. The humps don't form until the calves start eating solid food. That's when they begin to store fat in their humps. Even after a camel calf learns to eat plant foods, it drinks its mother's milk until it is at least a year old. It stays close to its mother until it is an adult, at around five years of age.

This newborn dromedary already has very long legs!

How Have People Used Camels?

Because camels could carry heavy loads and needed little water, they were the main pack animals on the *Silk Road*. This long, dangerous trade route was used to carry silk and other prized goods between China and the Mediterranean Sea.

Camel dung burns well. Its low flame burns for a long time and doesn't make much smoke.

Domesticated camels were very important to people living in desert regions of Asia and Africa. Bactrians were used mostly to carry goods. Dromedaries were important for work and also for riding. Why did people rely on camels so heavily? Because these animals were big and tough. They could live in places that were too hot and dry for horses and cattle.

A big camel can carry up to 1,000 pounds (454 kg)—although an easier load might be closer to 330 pounds (150 kg). Camels don't walk fast, but they can walk a long way, day after day. In the days before cars, they were perfect for carrying goods or people on long trips. Many people who raised camels also used their meat, milk, and skins. They used camel hair to make cords, cloth, rugs, tents, and paint brushes. In some areas, people burned camel *dung*, or body waste, as fuel.

This camel is helping to harvest sugarcane in Egypt.

People tried bringing camels to other hot, dry regions, such as Spain and the American Southwest. Most of these attempts failed. But Bactrians and dromedaries taken to Australia in the 1800s and early 1900s did well. They were used for riding, exploring unknown regions, pulling wagons, and carrying goods. In the 1920s and 1930s, cars and trucks took over most of the camels' jobs. But many camels had escaped or been set free. With no natural enemies, the camel population started to grow. And it has kept on growing! Nobody knows exactly how many camels there are in Australia today. People think there are well over 500,000—maybe closer to a million.

These dromedaries live in Australia.

Wild animals have never belonged to people. **Feral animals once belonged to people but got loose. Australia's camels are feral.**

During World War I, Australian, British, and New Zealand troops formed the Imperial Camel Corps. They rode camels to war in the Egyptian desert.

In some rugged regions, camels are still used to pull plows and wagons and to carry people and goods. Camel herders still live in some areas, including parts of the Gobi Desert. These people still live as nomads, moving with their camels from place to place.

In other regions, people enjoy camels more as reminders of the past—and for racing! Camel racing is a popular sport in some Middle Eastern countries. The camels can run as fast as 40 miles (65 km) an hour. Many racing camels are slim, with small humps. The riders sit either in front of or behind the hump.

These camels are racing during a festival in India.

In parts of Asia, camels were used in wars well into the 1900s.

In many places, camel rides are popular with tourists.

Camel milk tastes slightly saltier than cow's milk, but it's rich and nutritious. It can be used to make yogurt, butter, and soft cheese.

25

How Do Wild Camels Live?

Camels have been known to swim.

Camels are very smart. They have good eyesight and hearing and a good sense of smell.

Camels make lots of different sounds. They roar and bellow. They moan and groan. They make high bleating sounds and odd rumbles.

People have studied camels roaming free in Australia. Even though these camels came from domesticated ones, they have gone back to their wild ways. They live in groups of 2 to 20, with a male leader, one to several females, and some young. Other males live by themselves or in groups of males. In dry weather, hundreds of animals might come together, moving around to find water.

Wild Bactrian camels also live in groups. Some 6 to 30 females and young camels might live in a group led by an adult male. Other wild Bactrians live alone.

This herd of wild Bactrian camels lives in Mongolia.

Are Camels in Danger?

Camels can live for up to 50 years.

The Gobi desert is a difficult environment. Scientists have a lot to learn about how wild Bactrians can survive there.

Some people have been trying to cross camels with llamas, to grow llamas' fine wool on a bigger animal. The first camel-llama baby, called a *cama*, was named Rama.

There are millions of domesticated camels in the world, most of them dromedaries. There are no truly wild dromedaries anymore—only the feral ones in Australia. And there are fewer than a thousand wild Bactrians still living in Mongolia and China. These wild Bactrians are **endangered**. Governments and groups of people are working to protect areas of the Gobi Desert where the wild Bactrians live. They are also studying the Bactrians and raising young ones that will grow up to run free.

We know that domesticated camels will survive. And if we are successful at saving the areas where the wild Bactrians live, they will survive, too!

28

You can see the woolly fur on this young Bactrian camel.

Glossary

breeds (BREEDZ) Breeds are different types of an animal, developed by people choosing which males and females can have babies. There are many different breeds of camels.

calves (KAVZ) Calves are the young of some kinds of animals, such as cows or elephants. Baby camels are called calves, too.

domesticated (duh-MESS-tih-kay-tud) Animals that are domesticated are controlled and kept by people. Camels have been domesticated for thousands of years.

endangered (en-DAYN-jurd) An endangered animal is one that is close to dying out completely. Wild Bactrian camels are endangered.

environment (en-VY-run-ment) An environment is the kind of place in which a plant or animal lives, including the land, other plants and animals, water, and weather. Extreme temperatures and lack of water make the Gobi Desert a difficult, dangerous environment.

feral (FER-ull) A feral animal is one that has gotten away from its owners and gone wild. Australia has at least half a million feral camels.

mammals (MAM-ullz) Mammals are warm-blooded animals that have hair on their bodies and feed their babies milk from the mother's body. Camels are mammals.

nomadic (noh-MA-dik) Nomadic means moving from place to place as a way of life, rather than settling in one spot. Some camel herders are nomadic.

nutritious (noo-TRIH-shuss) Nutritious foods have lots of substances that animals' bodies need to stay strong and healthy. Camel's milk is nutritious.

saliva (suh-LY-vuh) Saliva is a liquid in animals' mouths that helps them chew, swallow, and break down food. Camels sometimes "spit" a mixture of thrown-up food and saliva.

steppes (STEPS) Steppes are dry grasslands. Bactrian camels came from the steppes of Asia.

tourists (TUR-ists) Tourists are people who visit an area to sightsee. In desert lands, tourists often want to try riding a camel.

To Find Out More

Read It!

Barnes, Julia. *Camels and Llamas at Work*. Milwaukee, WI: Gareth Stevens, 2006.

García, Eulalia, and Gabriel Casadevall and Ali Garousi (illustrators). *Camels: Ships of the Desert*. Milwaukee, WI: Gareth Stevens, 1996.

Wexo, John Bonnett. *The Camel Family* (Zoobooks). San Diego, CA: Wildlife Education, Ltd., 1999.

On the Web

Visit our Web page for lots of links about camels:
http://www.childsworld.com/links

Note to Parents, Teachers, and Librarians: We routinely check our Web links to make sure they're safe, active sites—so encourage your readers to check them out!

31

Index